A Special Gift To:

From:

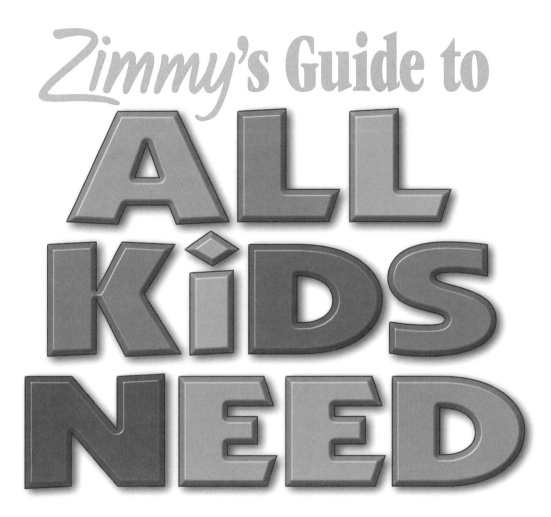

Zimmy's Guide to ALL KIDS NEED

New York, NY

This publication is sold with the intent to provide some helpful ideas, motivation and inspiration, in a generalized form. It is made available with the understanding that the author and publisher are not herein engaged in rendering psychological, legal or other professional advice or services. If expert assistance or counseling is needed, the services of a public or private agency, competent professional, or clergyperson should be sought.

Manufactured in Canada
00 01 02 03 04 05 06 07 TRC 10 9 8 7 6 5 4 3 2 1

Publisher's Cataloging-in-Publication:
Zimberg, Zimmy.
Zimmy's guide to all kids need : how all caring adults can nurture children /
by Zimmy Zimberg.
 -- 1st ed.
p. cm.
ISBN: 1-928995-00-4
Library of Congress Card Number: 00-190991

1. Child rearing. 2. Child welfare. I Title.

HQ769.Z56 2000   649.1

Life's Great! Inc.
2565 Broadway, PMB #137
New York, NY 10025-5657

Write us! info@zimmy.net

Visit our web site! www.zimmy.net

Dedicated to:

My Parents
Donald & Shirley Zimberg
Who teach me Love

My Siblings
Marvin, Jerry, Steven
Leonard, Sarah & Dena
& their spouses & children
Who teach me Life

And to my Teacher
Reb Shlomo Carlebach
of blessed memory
Who taught me Soul

To Our Youth Belong the Future

*

Open your hearts sweetest friends!

One morning a child somewhere wakes up late. His father says "You are so stupid. Can't you do anything right?" His mother says "You always wake up late. No breakfast for you. You missed the bus. Hurry up and I'll take you to school. I'm embarrassed that you're my child." When he arrives at school, his teacher says, "Class, here's Robert, late again. He probably does that to get attention; just ignore him."

Is it any wonder if such a child grows up as a war monger, taking out his anger on every one and every thing?

Somewhere else that very morning, another child wakes up late, as well. His father says, "Good morning my sweet child. It is late. When you get home today, let's talk about ways we can work together to make sure you are on time in the future, because we care about you and want you to get the most out of school." His mother says, "Good morning sweet son. Though it is late, I've made you some delicious food to eat in the car. You're so important to us, let's work together on being more prompt." His teacher says, "Good morning Robert! It is so wonderful to have you and all the other dear children in our classroom. The earlier each of you come, the more time we have to enjoy your presence."

Is it any wonder if such a child grows up as a peace monger, sharing his love with others to make this world a little bit better?

- Adapted from a teaching of Reb Shlomo Carlebach

Dear Sweet Friend:

Standing in line one day, I observed a small, delicate infant crying in his mothers arms, possibly from the long wait, or the heat, or because he was in need of feeding. I was moved by the mother's soft, nurturing voice as she gently tried to comfort her baby, when an older man said angrily: "If that was *my* child, I would whip it right here, right now. When my baby was born, I whipped it there in the crib until it learned to cry no more."

I am honored that you have chosen to read my book, which is written in defiance of that abusive man with the whip... and in defiance of *any* child abuse, neglect or maltreatment, wherever it is found. I do not profess to have all the answers to the difficult questions of how to raise and care for children. You might not agree with everything presented here. But one thing I'm sure you'll agree with, is that it starts with love and compassion.

The voice of this book is directed at parents and guardians, and many of the suggestions are appropriate for them alone. Nonetheless, many of the ideas presented here will also be relevant to grandparents, caregivers, educators, counselors, youth leaders, babysitters, administrators, health professionals, clergy, legislators, and any other adult who cares deeply about children and youth. Naturally, please use common sense to adapt the suggestions to fit your *particular* situation, relationship with a child, values and personal style.

None of us are perfect; we all make mistakes along the way. But we can each feel capable, act confidently, and try our best. Whatever your role, you have so much to offer, so many unique contributions to make in the life of a child!

If this book helps advocate for more love and compassion for children, I will feel immensely privileged. For *"The proof that God has not given up on the world is found in the face of a child."* How awesome are the opportunities we have as adults, to touch the lives of children in positive and wondrous ways!

With much love,   *Zimmy*

PS: I greatly value your input and welcome your comments. Please keep in touch! E-mail me at zimmy@zimmy.net or write to: Zimmy Zimberg, Life's Great! • 2565 Broadway PMB #137 • New York, NY 10025-5657

All Kids Need:

A Peaceful Home ❦ Acceptance ❦ Art, Dance, Music & Drama
Bedtime Stories ❦ Caring Adults ❦ Celebrations
Communication ❦ Community ❦ Compliments & Praise
Discipline ❦ Education ❦ Encouragement ❦ Family
Forgiveness ❦ Freedom for Creativity & Imagination
Gentleness ❦ Goals ❦ Good Medical Care & Treatment
Healthy, Nutritious Food ❦ Healthy Self Esteem & Self Worth
Help with Homework ❦ Honesty & Integrity
Hope for a Bright & Beautiful Tomorrow ❦ Hugs
Individuality ❦ Joy & Laughter ❦ Kindness ❦ Life Skills
Listening ❦ Motivation ❦ Mourning Losses ❦ Nature
No Abuse, Insult, Neglect, Maltreatment or Manipulation
Non-judgmental Validation of Emotions & Feelings
Nurturance ❦ Opportunities for Exploration & Discovery
Opportunities to Make Mistakes, Fall & Get Back Up
Patience ❦ Personal Space & Privacy ❦ Play ❦ Positivity
Protection ❦ Quality Time ❦ Quiet Time ❦ Respect
Responsibilities & Rules ❦ Role Models & Ethical Heroes
Safe, Secure Homes & Schools ❦ Spirituality
Sports & Exercise ❦ Structure & Order ❦ Sufficient Sleep
Support ❦ Togetherness ❦ Tolerance & Understanding
Toys & Treats (...but not too many sweets)
Trust ❦ Unconditional Love ❦ Values, Ethics & Character
Wholesome Friends ❦ X-tra Loving & Attention
Yes More Than No ❦ Zany Zebras with Purple Polkadots
& Lots of Other Silly Things to Laugh About Together!

Zimmy Zimberg

All Kids Need:
A Peaceful Home

*

Be a peacemaker! A home filled with strife breeds anger, resentment and unrest, while a home filled with peace promotes understanding, forgiveness and tranquility.

Each family member has different perspectives, different needs. Learn, teach and model the art of peacemaking in your home. Practice good communication and conflict resolution skills with your spouse and child ... positive skills that will be used effectively outside the home, as well.

When encountering differences, work on listening and coming up with solutions and compromise, rather than fighting or arguing. Disagree without insulting, invalidating or putting down. Don't take sides unfairly. Don't "dump" adult disagreements on your kids.
If facing separation or divorce, be civil about the process (and explain to your children they are not to blame for your decision).

Strive to promote understanding and tolerance. Make your house a home, a place of respite, refuge and comfort from what can often be a tough world out there.

Try It!
Action: At the next family disagreement, use understanding and good communication to come up with a peaceful solution.

All Kids Need:
Acceptance

*

All kids need acceptance. Who doesn't?

Imagine if – in the eyes of those you care about most –
you never make the grade.... you are never good enough...
everything you do falls short of their expectations.
You'd feel pretty bad about yourself.

Acceptance means: You do not need to be perfect.

Even when you make mistakes or do foolish things...
still, I love and accept you unconditionally.
Without any if's or but's.
Without any strings or conditions attached.

Try It!
Tell your child today:
"I think you're wonderful... just as you are.
I'm so glad you're you!"

All Kids Need:
Art, Dance, Music & Drama

✳

Yes, language, math, science and social studies are indeed essential for children, as these teach cognitive skills that will be applied throughout their lives. But creative skills are also critical to the developmental needs of a child.

Art, dance, movement, music and drama allow a child to feel, experience and express. They help sharpen a child's skills of observing, perceiving and discovering.

Cultural experiences broaden and deepen a child's insights, attention to detail and nuance, and appreciation of balance and harmony.

Encourage your child's school to provide opportunities for art, dance, music and drama. And make your own home a place where your child can paint, sculpt, draw, dance, move, play an instrument, sing, hum... and experience the beauty and vitality of the human spirit!

Try It!
Take your child to a museum, play or concert. Afterwards share your thoughts and feelings on the experience.

All Kids Need:
Bedtime Stories

✳

My fondest memories of childhood may include hot
chocolate with whipped cream, warm fudge cookies,
and ice cream with sprinkles...

But perhaps best of all were the times when Mom or Dad or
a sibling or babysitter would read to me just before I went to sleep,
especially from Aesop's Fables and books about heroes.

Besides being a great incentive to get kids to brush their teeth and
get into their pajamas, reading at bedtime provides other benefits,
as well, including: quality time for bonding, enhanced imagination,
development of literacy skills, and a wonderful prelude
to sweet dreams for the rest of the night!

As your child gets older, bedtime is also a great time
to listen to her read.

Try It!
**Try to read to your child at least
three times during the week ahead.**

All Kids Need:
Caring Adults

✳

Fact is: children left by themselves will perish.
Children, by nature, must rely on adults to take care of their needs.

The primary providers of these needs are parents.
But it is the extended responsibility of *all* adults in society to be
attuned to children's needs, and to help share and offer support in the
provision of their food, shelter, health, safety, education, and love.

Everyone can help, either directly by assisting parents, volunteering,
foster parenting or adopting, or indirectly by donating to
organizations that service the needs of children and youth.

For every child is – on some level – your child and mine.

As they mature, we give children "wings" by imbuing them with
the skills and confidence to be more and more independent.
They then can grow into adults responsible for themselves,
and capable of caring for the next generation of youth,
in the ongoing cycle of life.

Try It!
Contribute to an organization that helps
meet the needs of children and youth.
Even consider fostering or adopting a child.

All Kids Need:
Celebrations

✳

As adults, we can get so busy with the chores and responsibilities of life,
that we pass by opportunities to stop and
celebrate the here and now, the accomplishments.

How wonderfully rewarding it is to children
when parents throw even a simple birthday party for them,
or who show up at a school play, science fair, little league game,
or other occasion that they are a part of.

Life is short, and is not always so easy or simple.
So take every opportunity to Celebrate!
Take plenty of photos and videos!
Invite family and friends to be part of life-cycle events.

Together enjoy and express gratitude for
the simple pleasures and joys of life.

Try It!
With your child, plan a small, simple and
inexpensive "Celebration of Life and Love"
for your family and loved ones.

All Kids Need:
Communication

*

No one can know what is in someone else's head or heart unless that person *communicates*. Some kids are better at verbal communication while others do better in written form.
For some, communication comes easy, for others it is a challenge.

Help your child learn the art of communication:

To express his feelings and thoughts, joys and frustrations, and not keep things all wrapped up inside.

To utilize tools of negotiation and assertiveness, rather than aggressiveness or manipulation.

To be alert and aware of other people's verbal and non-verbal communication.

To be sensitive to other people's needs and know how to respond.

Communication also means giving your child cues about how you or other members of the family are feeling, such as "I've had a very tough day today; I'd be so proud of you if you would please help me out by playing a bit more quietly just now."

Try It!
Role play with your child, simulating various real-life social scenes. Practice how she might effectively respond in different situations.

All Kids Need:
Community

*

*

The oft-repeated Native American maxim of "It takes a village to raise a child" has special resonance these days. In the past, kids often benefitted from closer extended families, with grandparents, uncles, aunts and other relatives helping parents in the difficult task of parenting.

These days are different. With so many conflicting roles and responsibilities, media and technology competing for our attention, increasing problems of drugs and violence, parents and kids can benefit from Community. This can mean your neighborhood, your school, your place of worship, youth groups, parent support, local agencies or any other gathering of people who respect and care about each other.

Les Brown tells us that he didn't get involved in the drugs and gangs so readily available to him as a youth, because of a caring woman in the neighborhood. She would whisper in his ear, "Why get involved with all that, when someone as smart as you can have such a promising future!"

These days, we all have to look out for each other's children.

Try It!
Discuss with your child which relatives and neighbors she should feel comfortable turning to in times of trouble.

All Kids Need:
Compliments & Praise

✳

Tell a child everything that's wrong with her... and watch her sour.

Tell a child you are so very proud of her... and watch her soar!

Try these:
"You are so very special"
"You made the right choice!"
"I see you've tried very hard"
"Good for you!"
"I'm so proud of you!"
"Way to go!"
"You are so smart!"
"And you did it all by yourself!"
"Teach me how to do that!"

(PS: The more specific a compliment is,
the more meaningful it will be to your child.)

Try It!
**Find one especially good thing about your child
each day, and tell him about it!**

All Kids Need:
Discipline

*

Discipline is about teaching a child self-discipline,
a skill that is essential to most every aspect of life. It is about
teaching a child responsibility and consequences for his actions.

Discipline is *never* about taking one's own anger or frustrations out
on a child, nor about causing undue suffering or embarrassment.
If you yourself are getting overwhelmed, take a walk, call a friend.

Because even as adults, our own emotions can be volatile and
consequently hurtful, discipline must be balanced with benevolence.
Take charge in a firm but fair way. Let your child know that you will not
tolerate certain behaviors and attitudes, and that – for children as well as
adults – choices have consequences. Keep your credibility by being
consistent and following through. Set a good example by living the
behavior you expect from your children. For example, if you expect them
not to use foul language, then you must follow the same rules, as well.

While not every decision you hand down need be explained,
explanations will help your child learn to formulate and
apply her own skills of self-discipline.

Try It!
**The next time you must discipline your child,
first stop and think:
what is the most effective approach?**

All Kids Need:
Education

*

Take part in your child's education.

School administrators, board members and teachers expend much energy trying to make a positive difference in the lives of the children in their care. They aren't perfect. But they do mean well and welcome your input and suggestions, especially when those are made constructively and with good will, rather than with animosity. They also welcome your participation – in parent-teacher conferences, PTA/PTO, board meetings, and volunteering.

Give them compliments and offer your thanks, as their jobs are not always so easy.

Education does not stop in the formal confines of school, but continues in all aspects of a child's life.

Challenge your child to be inquisitive and always yearning to learn from people and the world around him. In learning about life, there are no "stupid" questions.

Try It!
Write your child's teachers a short note telling them how much you appreciate their efforts and talents as an educator.

All Kids Need:
Encouragement

*

We all thrive on encouragement.

Tell a kid that you believe in them,
and they will start believing in themselves.

"You can do it!"
"Give it your best shot!"
"I'm behind you all the way!"
"I know you have what it takes"
"Give it a try, even if you fail"
"You are so capable!"
"I believe in you!"

Praise is the most potent motivator.
Try some today!

Try It!
**Come up with your own list of 10 words
of encouragement and praise.
Use them generously with your child.**

All Kids Need:
Family

*

Family is about acceptance, support and unconditional love.

But a strong, close family doesn't just happen.
It takes a lot of attention and effort to develop, nurture and
build the love, appreciation and compassion that are the
foundations of a strong, supportive family:

"Let's call Grandma today!"
"Wow! Look how much your brother cares about you!"
"Tell your sister you're sorry for hurting her feelings."
"Your father has had a tough day... he could use a hug."
"Your brother just got accepted into the school band...
wish him congratulations on his accomplishment!"
"What can we plan special for Mother's Day to
thank Mom for everything she does for us?"
"Aunt Karen is coming over for the weekend, it would be so
nice if you'd offer her your bed while you sleep on the couch."
"Your sister is feeling sad after losing her dog...
she's going to need extra sensitivity from us all."
"No matter what happens, we're gonna stick together!"

Try It!
Hold regular family meetings, where tasks are
divvied up and family members can openly,
honestly express themselves without censure.

All Kids Need:
Forgiveness

*

One of the saddest dysfunctions of families is when members hold grudges for long periods of time.

Some family members haven't spoken to each other for years and years. Sometimes it is for good reason, as when it is needed to avoid a very hurtful person. But often grudges emanate from pride and stubbornness. Love is too precious to get caught in that kind of "life-stuckedness."

No one is perfect. We all make mistakes. Daily.

Don't let feuds and bad feelings fester in your home, but let compassion and forgiveness be the foundations of a peaceful home.

Teach your child to forgive others.

Forgive your child for his mistakes.

Try It!
**Tell your child "Watch this!"
Then, call up someone you have had a feud with, and ask her forgiveness.**

All Kids Need:
Freedom for Creativity & Imagination

✻

The "left-brain" (creative) part of ourselves is vital to our existence!

Not a single advancement, invention or breakthrough in civilization
would have been created had it not been for someone taking
a different road, a second look, a risk to try new ideas,
an adventure into unlimited possibilities.

Let every child be encouraged to explore and discover.

And, if your child is especially inquisitive,
that is a special gift and ability that should not be stifled,
but rather nurtured and nourished.

Try It!
Take your child on an impromptu, spontaneous
mystery ride. Objective: To discover five
new things about the world!

All Kids Need:
Gentleness

*

If your personality is a bit strong and bold...

If your job requires you to be very assertive...

If you are, by nature, very confident or intense...

Know that, at home,
strength is often found
in gentleness.

Don't be overzealous with reason.
Even if your view seems most logical,
emotions and feelings must also be considered.

Seek to affect change not through force or coercion,
but by the gentle strength of example and leadership.

Try It!
Try speaking to your child today in an especially warm and gentle tone.

All Kids Need:
Goals

*

It's so easy for a child to get overwhelmed with school, homework, family, friends, extra-curricular activities, chores and responsibilities.

Help your child learn the self-rewarding joy of setting goals and achieving them. (This is especially important for children with Attention Deficit Disorder or other learning differences.)

Small, realistic, short-term, achievable goals can help a child build self confidence and mastery.

Personal Progress charts are great... as long as expectations aren't too demanding, and rewards aren't far off.

Focus more on goals achieved than those missed.

Accentuate accomplishments.

Try It!
Together with your child, develop a chart that lists realistic daily objectives. Reward achievements.

All Kids Need:
Good Medical Care & Treatment

✳

Physical health plays no small role in the physical,
emotional and social development of a child.
It is every child's right to receive good medical care and treatment.

Good health ideas include:
Choose physicians and medical specialists wisely, by referrals from those you
trust. Keep an open dialog with your pediatrician. Don't be shy: ask
questions; solicit advice. Keep abreast of new medical advances. Search the
web for up-to-date information to help you make educated choices. Be sure
your child gets regular inoculations. If your child's doctor prescribes medica-
tion, keep on schedule. Practice healthy hygiene and germ control at home.
When pregnant, keep especially healthy, and avoid doing something foolish
that might harm your child.

Provide a healthy and safe environment for your child.

Have a policy of zero tolerance in your family for illegal drug use,
and alcohol and drug abuse. If *you* smoke, *now* is the time to stop.

Try It!
Talk with your kids – rather than lecture – about the
dangers of alcohol and drug abuse, and smoking. Help
them prepare for – and deal with – peer pressure.

All Kids Need:
Healthy, Nutritious Food

*

Fat content, sugar content, calories, fiber, cholesterol, etc.
are not concerns for adults only.

Indeed, healthy foods are vital to provide children with the nutrition
their bodies and minds need to grow strong, active and alert,
and to fend off illness and disease.

Avoid cereals and snack foods with high sugar content.
Cook with less fats and oils.
Be aware of food allergies.
Learn about the revised "food pyramid" of balanced nutrition.
Generally speaking, increase fruits, vegetables and whole grains
and decrease red meats and fatty foods.
Read labels; buy wisely.
Take a community class in preparing nutritious foods.
Encourage your family to eat fruits and other healthy snack foods.
Consider organic food options.
Encourage your family to eat in moderation.

Try It!
**Review your child's nutrition needs, and make
appropriate modifications for her maximum health.**

All Kids Need:
Healthy Self-Esteem & Self-Worth

*

There are actually three components to a child feeling good about herself: self-concept, self-esteem and self-worth.

Healthy *self-concept* means that when a child looks into the mirror, she feels good about her appearance, and says "I accept my weight, my height, my looks. I accept the type and style of dress that I can afford."

The entertainment, fashion and cosmetics industries make it difficult for kids & teens to accept anything less than perfection... as if there is such a thing! Anorexia and bulimia are especially destructive illnesses that affect some teens, and can be due to low self-concept.

*

Healthy *self-esteem* means that a child feels good about who he is, and says "I like myself. I am capable, intelligent, creative, etc." He has a realistic assessment of his abilities and disabilities, he generally loves and accepts himself, and he treats himself with respect and dignity.

Sometimes a controlling, manipulative or bullying child must be "put in his place" to realize that the world isn't centered on himself alone. While "difficult" or anti-social behavior can be a result of overinflated self-esteem, it can also be a way that a child tries to compensate for his low self-esteem.

It's tricky, because even though one's self-esteem should not necessarily be tied to achievement, often times healthy self-esteem does come from feeling capable, taking responsibility for oneself, accomplishing things, and enjoying the fruits of one's labors. A child who often fails may feel defeated.

Nurturing each child to develop areas of personal mastery and excellence, and setting and achieving small and realistic goals helps children (and adults!) build healthy self-esteem.

✻

Healthy *self-worth* means a child feels that she has value in the world, and says "I have unique and special contributions to make to society; I am wanted and needed, I have much to offer others. I matter."

The three components mentioned here are complex, with many contributing factors... some beyond our control. But there is a wealth of good that parents, teachers and other adults can do to nurture a child's positive and healthy feelings of self... which naturally lead to healthy relationships, as well.

Try It!
Help your child do a positive assessment of herself, writing down what makes her special and unique!

All Kids Need:
Help with Homework

✳

Homework might seem inconvenient, but it is a vital part of a child's academic and personal development, and an integral part of the responsibilities of parenting.

Be sure your child knows clearly what the homework assignments are.
Set a regular time and place for homework.
Provide an organized and clean workspace.
Be sure that the television is off and other distractions are minimized.

Don't do the work for your child, but be there to help, guide, challenge, encourage, motivate, and ease the frustration.
If you become aware of areas that your child might need extra assistance with, investigate tutoring options.

Homework may be a chore,
but it should never be a punishment.
Remember that the learning *process* is just as important as getting the right answers.

Try It!
Make sure your school-age child has a special "homework" notebook for assignments. (*FranklinCovey* makes excellent ones!)

All Kids Need:
Honesty & Integrity

*

It's amazing what kids pick up from their home lives.
If a child lives in an environment that values honesty, he will most likely retain that as an integral value throughout his life. True, he may now or later face negative influences and challenges. But there will always be that resonating voice, "In this family honesty is a prized virtue."

What matters most is not so much what adults say,
but how we act and set examples for kids.

You can even model how challenging it is at times to be honest, such as explaining in a real situation, "I feel like lying right now because it will save me from embarrassment, but I won't lie because I know it is wrong. I'd rather follow my conscience and tell the truth."
(Even that would be utmost honesty: letting your child know that bad temptations are normal, but acting on them would be wrong.

Above all, always be honest with your child.

Try It!
Discuss different life situations and moral dilemmas with your child, discussing what are honest and dishonest choices.

All Kids Need:
Hope for a Bright & Beautiful Tomorrow

*

Hope and faith are two of the key ingredients that keep
anyone – adult or child – buoyant and resilient
through the many difficulties and challenges of life.

Most children have a natural, innate sense of hope.
Cultivate and nurture that awesome characteristic.

If a child comes home feeling defeated,
help her cope with the pain... and look to the future.

If your family is going through loss, change, financial difficulty or crisis,
often it affects your child at least as much as it affects you.
Reassure your child – and your family – that you'll all stick together even
during tough times, and look to the future for bright things to come.

Try It!
**With your child, create a poem, song or picture
about hope, and refer to it when times are tough.**

All Kids Need:
Hugs

*

Touch is an important part of communication, and the warmth of expression that a hug brings can be wonderfully reassuring.

But there are good hugs and bad hugs.

Teach your child that there are good touches and bad touches, that her body is her own, and that she has the right to refuse a hug or kiss from anyone, even a relative or other adult they might know. Teach them what to do if approached by a stranger. Tell them to inform you if they are ever touched in a way that makes them feel bad or "dirty."

Nice ways to show affection to children might be a handshake, a warm smile, a reassuring hand on a shoulder, or a kiss on the forehead rather than on the lips or cheeks. In any event, all adults must behave with appropriate boundaries and respect the rights of every child.

Try It!
Discuss with your child the difference between good touches and bad touches.

All Kids Need:
Individuality

*

Just as no two fingerprints are alike, just as no two snowflakes are alike, the miracle of life is that no two children are alike.

Each child has different abilities and challenges, strengths and weaknesses. Each child has different cognitive and behavioral styles, different life experiences and points of reference. Each child has different needs, different things that they succeed or struggle with.

Rather than label a child with "disabilities" or "handicap," use words like "differences" and "special needs."

Don't compare siblings or classmates.
Honor differences and individuality.
Never favor one sibling over the next.

Your child is unique and special, and cannot be compared with anyone else in the entire world.

In fact, every one in life has something special to offer the world, that no one else can.

Try It!
Help your child create a book or journal, titled "Why I Am So Special!"

All Kids Need:
Joy & Laughter

＊

Sometimes adults get so wrapped up in the seriousness and
heaviness of life, that we forget to laugh and have fun
and just enjoy the simple pleasures of life.

Perhaps that's one of the reasons that God put children in the world...
to remind us not to take ourselves so seriously that we forget to
marvel at the sheer beauty and wonder of being alive.

After all, isn't it an amazing phenomenon
that it is nearly impossible not to laugh when a child laughs!

So, find lots of opportunities with children for
simple, spontaneous joy and laughter!

Try It!
**Read an age-appropriate children's joke book,
or book of riddles with your child. Enjoy!**

All Kids Need:
Kindness

*

As adults, we must be attuned to the needs of *all* children
in our communities, and go out of our way to
help make their lives happy and healthy.

If child is lost...
Needs help crossing the street...
Is frustrated...
Needs comforting...
Needs clothing or other basic needs...
Help out in meaningful and significant ways.

Kindness to children is also shown by reaching out to
their parents, offering assistance and moral support.

Especially for single parents, childrearing is not an easy job.
A helping hand to them is a generous act of kindness.

Try It!
Offer your help to a parent or teacher today.

All Kids Need:
Life Skills

*

There's an old saying: "A wise person learns from the mistakes of others while a fool waits to learn from his own mistakes."

No one has all the answers, but *together* we can share the life lessons, tools and skills we have learned – often times the hard way – to navigate through the difficult course of life, relationships, careers, etc.

In many schools, what used to be called "Home Economics" is now sometimes called "Life Management." To manage our lives is neither simple nor easy. But the earlier we give our children life management skills, the better chance they have at creating success in their lives.

Teach your child common sense skills of cooking, building, fixing, saving, organizing, swimming, ...and anything else that is practical and good to know.

Similarly, teach your child social skills of effective communication, anger management and conflict resolution. Roll-playing helps, too. After all, "social skills" are *skills* which can be taught and learned.

Try It!
Make a list of 10 practical things your child should know about navigating life and staying buoyant through its storms. Share this list, on his level.

All Kids Need:
Listening

*

The art of communication is a balance between expressing one's own self
and listening to another, of having something to say but
also wanting to hear what the other has to say.
Communication with children requires no less.

Whichever cynic said that "Children should be seen and not heard"
didn't begin to appreciate an ounce of the sacred wonder of infants,
children, youth and teens, nor what awesome things they teach us daily.
Moreover, how can we know what each kid needs,
if we don't take the time to listen. Intently. Deeply.

Imagine the effectiveness of parents who must confront their teen
on a difficult issue, and – instead of lecturing – broach the topic with
something like this: "Some people might say you need a good talking to.
I say that you need a good listening to!" What a marvelous show of
respect for this young adult as a person, and an invitation for her to
honestly, openly share some of the real pressures of being an adolescent.

Want to increase the chances that your kid won't turn to alcohol and
drugs? Build an open dialogue of respect and trust.

Try It!
**The next time your child does something wrong,
patiently ask him to explain what he did and why.
Guide him to come to the right conclusions.**

All Kids Need:
Motivation

*

We adults often look to all sorts of things to keep us focused and on track, such as inspiring quotations, posters, seminars, personal trainers, motivational speakers, self-help books, videos and tapes.

Children also need frequent and varied forms of motivation.

While praise is about how wonderful you feel your child is, motivation is about how much you believe in her, and then helping her muster the inner strength, perseverance, character and faith she'll need to make it through the obstacles and challenges.

From some adults, positive words might not come so easily. Maybe they feel it is too "mushy." Or perhaps they grew up with much criticism, and now find their *own* inner voice demanding, harsh, negative. If this resonates with you, I invite you to reach deep down inside and cultivate that part of yourself which is more positive, more nurturing. You and your child will benefit enormously.

Indeed, help your child develop his very *own* inner voice that resounds with an "I can do it!" attitude.

Try It!
**As you read this now, affirm to yourself:
"I'm a coach, not a drill sergeant."
"I'm a motivator, not a critic."**

All Kids Need:
Mourning Losses

*

Some parents – with good intentions – try to shield their children from the painful realities of loss and death.

One young friend of mine was never informed of his father's protracted terminal illness until he suddenly passed away one day. Another friend was sent away to camp as an alternative to being told of her mother's sudden death. The adults in her life just didn't know how to reveal the devastating news, they didn't want to crush this child with the awful truth. Instead, she learned of her mother's passing from her relatives two weeks later on the camp's visiting day.

With sincere intentions, we try to shield children from bad news.

But, just as adults, children also have the very human need to grieve, mourn, comfort and be comforted... all part of the healing process.

Try It!
When a loved one passes away or a pet dies, take the opportunity to discuss with your child her honest, painful feelings of loss and grief.

All Kids Need:
Nature

✳

Nature is deliciously nurturing!

Share opportunities with your children for communion with nature,
through family activities such as:
Bicycling
Trailblazing
Hiking
Gardening
Camping
Birdwatching
Stargazing
Leaf collecting
...and even a lazy Sunday afternoon picnic in the park.

Especially if you live in an urban area... get out of the "concrete jungle"
with your child and enjoy some nature.

Summer camp is also a wonderfully enriching experience
not to be missed by kids. Scholarships are often available.

Try It!
**Plan a family day at the park, zoo, aquarium,
botanical gardens or nature preserve near you.**

All Kids Need:

No Abuse, Insult, Neglect, Maltreatment or Manipulation

*

Sometimes abuse is done with intention to hurt, while other times it is done without malicious intent and awareness. Sometimes abuse is perpetrated by a total stranger, while other times it is perpetrated by someone known, such as a caretaker, neighbor or relative.

In any case, abuse and neglect of children or youth is cruel and criminal. It leaves physical and emotional scars that last a lifetime... and most often continue in a tragic cycle through future generations.

The most eloquent statement I've read is from a caring child advocate: "If I could change just one thing, I would stop people from beating their kids. Not just beating, but verbally abusing kids, neglecting kids. You lose your childhood when you've been abused. My heart goes out to those children who are abused and have no one to turn to.

"My wish is that children be treated as people, and not as property; that their rights as human beings on the planet – to food, shelter, education and health – be taken seriously. I see that the way people were treated as children causes them to grow up and behave certain ways as adults. I see it as the root of almost every problem in our society."

Physical abuse might include hitting, slapping, pushing, shaking.

Sexual abuse might include any sexual contact with a child, using a child for pornography, or exposing a child to adult sexual activity.

Emotional or verbal abuse might include put-downs, insults and threats.

Neglect might include failing to provide for a child's physical or emotional needs.

If you suspect your own child is being abused, seek help from your physician, mental health professional, or social services agency.

If you suspect abuse of *any* child, report the abuse to your local child protective, social services, or law enforcement agency.

If you yourself are saying or doing things that is hurting a child, stop it now. It is time to get professional help immediately. Children are not the dumping grounds for adults' problems.

Help your child learn the difference between good and bad touches, assertiveness skills, stranger danger, internet safety, what to do if they feel they've been touched in a bad or "dirty way," and who they can feel safe turning to and confiding in.

Together, with awareness, prevention, and determination, we have the power to end the devastating cycle of abuse.

Try It!
Consider if your words to your child are insulting or hurtful at times. Take a parenting class for more effective communication and discipline skills.

All Kids Need:

Non-judgmental Validation of Emotions & Feelings

✳

Every emotion and feeling we have is valid and genuine.
What matters is that we be aware of how we feel,
and then act in appropriate and healthy ways.

For example, anger is a real emotion.
A healthy response might be taking time to "cool off,"
or *appropriately* expressing our disappointment to the person who hurt us.
Likewise, frustration, embarrassment, sadness, etc. are all valid emotions.

Don't use invalidating statements like, "You don't mean that" or "You don't really feel that way." Instead, use empathetic statements such as "I feel sad that you feel hurt. I'm here for you." Let your child know they can always share their feelings honestly, without being judged.

Try It!
**With your child, identify 8 different emotions.
Explain that each is valid.
Discuss positive reactions to each.**

All Kids Need:
Nurturance

*

To grow, a seedling needs water, sunlight,
and protection from inclement weather.

To grow, kids needs love, support and nurturance.

To nurture means to provide those things that help a child grow,
such as positive, warm, and encouraging words.

On the other hand, sometimes in our sincere zeal to nurture,
we can become over-bearing, over-doting, or over-domineering.
It's like a plant that's been over-watered!
The secret – like all good things – is Balance.

Sometimes, what a child needs most to succeed
is to have one special adult in their lives
– a parent, grandparent, teacher, mentor or friend –
that cares about him,
believes in him,
offers him guidance,
and stands by him.

Try It!
**Diagnosis: Consider an area your child could use
an extra dose of nurturance from you.
Prescription: Apply generously!**

All Kids Need:
Opportunities for Exploration & Discovery

✳

Hodding Carter quotes a wise old woman who once said,
"There are only two lasting bequests we can hope to give our children.
One of these is roots, the other, wings."

Parenting and teaching is about a balance between
showing on the one hand, and letting a child learn on her own.

Give your child the thirst to learn and explore... and the skills of
inquiry, investigation, observation, analysis and evaluation.

Don't be afraid to give your kids wings.

Learn to let go.

Try It!
Find yourself saying to your child more frequently,
"Hmmm... why do you think this is?" and
"Hey, would you like to try this yourself?"

All Kids Need:
Opportunities to Make Mistakes, Fall & Get Back Up

*

Part of learning to be responsible and independent is being allowed to slip up and make mistakes.

Teach your child resiliency by showing him that making mistakes is o.k., especially when we learn from our mistakes.

Teach your child that the greatest successes in life often come on the heels of misfortune, failure and disappointment. Indeed, accomplishment *requires* mistakes along the way, in the process of refinement.

Let excellence be the benchmark; never perfection. Teach your child to listen to that inner voice which patiently says: If I fall, I can get right back up again.

Try It!
Review with your child a "mistake" you have made, and together extract the lessons to be learned.

All Kids Need:
Patience

*

If making mistakes and being imperfect is about our humanity,
then learning patience is about our humility.

The folk wisdom of our culture is filled with sayings such as
"Patience is a virtue" or "If at first you don't succeed, try try again."
(Our forebears knew what they were talking about!)

In fact, if we take a close look at anger – the emotion that wreaks
havoc in so many homes – we will see that it is the emotion
we feel when things do not go as we might want or expect.

Teach your child to put in good effort...
but not to hold too tightly to her expectation of the outcome.
Teach your child to try, but to let go of the tendency to control.
Teach your child to allow the mystery of life to
give meaning and reason to our efforts, even when things
don't go exactly as planned or hoped for.

Teach your child patience: with others, and with her own self.

Try It!
**The next time you are about to "explode" in anger,
turn to your child, smile, and gleefully say,
"I'm practicing patience!"**

All Kids Need:
Personal Space & Privacy

*

We as adults need to respect that
just because kids are kids,
doesn't mean that they also don't have
a sense of modesty
and need for privacy.

Don't embarrass your kid in public;
if you need to have a stern or revealing talk,
always do it in private.

Also, teach brothers and sisters to respect the personal space
and property of their siblings, by saying things like:
"Ask if you can play with his toys."
"Knock before you enter."
"Your sister is sleeping; let's play quietly."

Try It!
**Make it a family policy to knock on a
bedroom or bathroom door before entering,
to show respect for privacy.**

All Kids Need:
Play

*

What would childhood be without play?

And what would adulthood be for someone who
hadn't had abundant opportunity to play as a child?

Let your kid play... and join in on the fun!

These days, many toys have become too mechanized, with little
personal interaction, or too commercial, with tie-ins to movies and
television figures that children quickly become bored with. When buying
toys, choose those that have enduring value, and offer the most
opportunity for personal creativity, imagination and socialization.

My father always encourages our family to play cards, chess, checkers,
dominos and other board games, because they provide opportunities for
face-to-face interaction with family members young and old. What a
delight it is to watch Grandma Ida play with her great-grandchildren!

Always promote honesty, fairness, and equal opportunity,
with the goal of having fun together, rather than simply winning.

Try It!
Schedule a "Family Play Night"
with the type of games, skits, puzzles, riddles, etc.
that can increase family bonding.

All Kids Need:
Positivity

*

A mentor of mine once remarked: An adult can look out the window at a common, natural rainfall and say "What a bad day! I hope it stops raining," and a child learns to see the negative. Or, the adult can instead view the exact same scene and remark, "Wow! Look at how the trees and plants and bushes and flowers are all being watered right now!"
After all, we *do* need rainwater just as we need sunshine.

Teach your child to generally view "the glass"
as half-full rather than half-empty.

This is not to suggest denial of bad feelings nor to deny tough times and challenges. After all, the "floods" and "fires" of our lives should evoke feelings of pain and loss. But overall, having an attitude of gratitude to see and enjoy the beauty of life, promotes contentedness and resiliency.

Teach your child even to look for the positive benefits of the adversity and struggle that he will undoubtedly face throughout his life.
Help him to see problems as opportunities for growth.

Try It!
Next time you catch yourself being overly negative in front of your child, stop and turn it into a positive.

All Kids Need:
Protection

*

Life has its share of tough things.
Some are natural, like hurricanes and earthquakes. Some are accidental or due to negligence, like injuries and car accidents. Some are a result of insensitivity and irresponsibility, like when people do hurtful things, intentionally or not. And some things are out of fear, selfishness, or even cruelty, like violence, drug dealing and child molestation.

The challenge for caring adults is to protect children and youth from bad things, without being over-protective. Let your child know that not every thing in life is pretty, and not every person's actions are good.

Teach her self-reliance and self-preservation skills.
To be aware and alert of things that signal trouble.
To think for herself and not be swayed by pressure or manipulation.
To know who to turn to in times of trouble.
To know safety precautions and emergency procedures.

Keep a safe home: with fire alarms, electrical wiring up to code, medicines in child resistant containers, poisons far out of reach, and sockets covered from infants and toddlers. Practice common sense safety.

Try It!
Schedule "Our Home is a Safe Home" meetings on a quarterly basis to discuss safety habits and emergency procedures with your family.

All Kids Need:
Quality Time

*

These days, with an increased number of dual-working parents and single parents, time is an especially precious commodity. There are so many things competing for our time and attention.

Make sure to keep your child a top priority.

Quality time means: Turn off the t.v. and computer. Let your answering machine handle incoming phone calls. Give your undivided attention. Be emotionally present. Take real interest, rather than being nosey. Ask personal, specific questions, such as "What project did you do in Science class today?" or "How did you decide to handle that disagreement you had with your friend yesterday?"

Rituals, traditions and family meals can also serve as a framework for quality time spent together. Story telling and singing are excellent ways to build connection. Attending church or synagogue as a family can provide time together that is meaningful and inspiring.

Even when difficult, try to spend some quality time with each child. Tune in to each child's *individual* needs and interests.

Try It!
**Plan a relaxing vacation away from home.
Agree to just "chill out together,"
leaving behind technology and tension.**

All Kids Need:
Quiet Time

*

Some kids live in environments that are always busy, such as a home with lots of siblings or guests, or where there is a home business. Some kids live in environments that are always noisy, such as living in the hub-bub of urban life. Some kids live in environments that are always fast-paced, such as with parents who are professionals, executives or just "high-energy" by nature.

As night time arrives, set the mood by saying "Now is quiet time: when the pace slows down, when we give extra respect to family members and neighbors who might already be sleeping, when we prepare our own bodies and minds for a good nights rest."

Quiet and even solitude – at the right times – are important to promote inner peace, personal reflection, and tranquility in children and adults.

Try It!
Make sure your child gets opportunities for quiet, peaceful times, and a good night's sleep.

All Kids Need:
Respect

*

Kids are people, too! Children are entitled to respect. Their thoughts, feelings, ideas, and needs are valid and important. Respect differences. Adults think differently than children. Boys think differently than girls. Younger kids think differently than older kids. And one child might think differently than the next. When we respect our commonalities and differences, we are open to understanding and learning from each other.

Nobody likes to be lectured to. Don't dwell on the negative. When you need to point out a mistake, do so in a way that respects your child's integrity. Set rules & limits, but be reasonable and explain.

Ask "What is your opinion?" This is especially important with teens, who are bombarded with conflicting messages and values, and need guidance as they process their thoughts and feelings, and develop their unique identities. Don't try to "be" their minds. Don't be the "I told you so" voice of guilt. Rather, be a caring guide, a source of solid values and wisdom.

Ultimately, we are not our children. Help your child develop his values and skills of discernment so that he can arrive at good conclusions (even if those are different from the conclusions you might have made).

Try It!
Value your child's opinion. Increasingly ask, "What do you think?" "What is your opinion?"

All Kids Need:
Responsibilities & Rules

✳

Cleaning One's Room.
Household Chores.
Curfews.
Allowance.
Caring for pets.
Babysitting.

These age-appropriate activities help kids build character traits such as responsibility, integrity and compassion. They also help build that marvelous quality of self efficacy, which says, "If I want to accomplish something, I need to invest planning, hard work, energy, persistence, mindfulness and focus to achieve my goals."

Never make household chores into punishments, but as part of the contributions everyone makes to home and family. Similarly, make rules not as a show of force, but because they are sensible, practical, necessary and just. Encourage pride in one's work, however "mundane" or boring it might seem.

Try It!
To promote appreciation and gratitude, try a "switch" day where each family member shares a chore usually done by another.

All Kids Need:
Role Models & Ethical Heroes

✳

There might seem to be a shortage of positive role models.
But they are out there: in our neighborhoods, in our schools, in our
communities, in our churches, synagogues, mosques and temples.

Show your child – by your words and actions – that the most important
people in the world are not necessarily famous, wealthy or of celebrity...
but simple people who are good and honest and courageous,
and quietly go out of their way for others each and every day:

The shopkeeper who immediately hands back extra change to any
customer who mistakenly overpays. The senior adult, advanced in years,
who works hard to maintain his flower garden in the public courtyard to
bring cheer to others. The clergy person who gives wise guidance and
counsel to others, helping them to unload their burdens, without
expectation of payment or honor. The student who – even though
burdened with her own school work – devotes several hours a week
as a tutor and mentor to less fortunate students in the neighborhood.

Try It!
**Find some local heroes and – with your child –
celebrate them in some special way, in your home,
school, or community center.**

All Kids Need:
Safe, Secure Homes & Schools

*

Have you seen a child who is growing up in fear?
It is so sad, leaving emotional scars that last a lifetime
and often continue into successive generations.

Fighting and arguing in the home traumatizes.
Drugs and alcohol in our neighborhoods ruin lives.
Guns and violence in our schools kill.
War devastates.

Is your child – or your neighbor's child – growing up in fear?
If so, don't be complacent or silent. Do something about it:
Report unhealthy living standards to local authorities.
If necessary, complain until a positive solution is found.
Join a children's advocacy group.
Be part of your school's "Safe & Drug Free" committee.
Get involved in school and local politics.
Contribute to a charity serving the most needy of children.
Launch an *"All Kids Need"* parent support group.

Try It!
Be an advocate for the safety and security of children... on a local, national or global level.

All Kids Need:
Spirituality

*

There are many forms of expression of spirituality.
Whether you believe in God or struggle with the concept, whether you
observe the tenets of your religion or create your own unique rituals,
spirituality is about our search for meaning and divine connectivity.

Let your child experience the joys of spirituality,
and the happiness found in living life in harmony with
the highest ideals of his soul, or conscience.

Observe not only the rules and traditions of your heritage,
but also learn about and celebrate its beauty and wisdom.

Respect your child's needs for her own individual religious expression.

Teach respect and tolerance for people of *all* faiths.
For ultimately, our appreciation of Something far greater than ourselves
is a source of oneness, humility, and love for all.

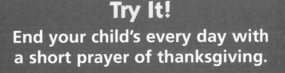

Try It!
**End your child's every day with
a short prayer of thanksgiving.**

All Kids Need:
Sports & Exercise

*

Common wisdom says that sports is not about winning or losing, but rather "how you play the game."

Sports teach us teamwork, self-discipline, good health, balance, focus, exerted effort, stamina, persistence, fairness, playing by the rules, and so many other important values.

A good parent or coach will encourage each child according to her own individual capacity, help her build a competitive edge, yet acknowledge effort and teamwork as far more important end-goals than winning.

Exercise – especially aerobic – is great not only for muscle tone, but for alertness and stress reduction. Activities such as running, swimming, bicycling, etc. help one's heart and lungs function at healthier capacity. Exercise can be especially important for children with hyperactivity, or for those who flourish best with less competitive activities.

Make sure your child has plenty of opportunities to participate in sports and exercise, to help him channel his energy in healthy, positive ways.

Try It!
Invite your child to join you on an invigorating, early morning brisk walk, jog or run.

All Kids Need:
Structure & Order

*

A child who lives life in disorder and chaos is more likely to have problems with low productivity, procrastination, low tolerance of frustration, and the poor self esteem that often follows.

Cleanliness and orderliness, on the other hand, allow for a peaceful spirit, high productivity, sustained focus, mindfulness, and healthy self esteem that flow from getting things done well and on time.

Help your child learn good time management skills.
Help him keep an orderly, organized bedroom.
Make sure she has a clean, well-lit study area.
Develop a schedule and reward her for keeping to it.
Make sure he has the right tools for school, including
notebooks that help keep school work categorized.
Encourage her to select clothes and lunch each night before
school days, to reduce morning stress and promote preparedness.

Try It!
Review your child's physical space.
Get shelving and organizers as necessary
to help make his life more orderly.

All Kids Need:
Sufficient Sleep

*

Ask the school teachers!
Every one of them will tell us that a child who comes to school after
having had a good night's rest is more likely to be alert, refreshed,
energized, and in a good mood to start the day right.

Ask the parents!
Every one of them will tell us that a child who hasn't had a good night's
rest, (and a daytime nap), can be cranky, moody, and near intolerable.

Make sure your child has
a good mattress,
clean sheets,
a comfortable pillow,
a small night light,
and – most important –
a peaceful home that is conducive to
a good night's rest.

Try It!
End each of your child's days with words of
gentleness and love, such as "Sweetest dreams
my dear... I love you so much!"

All Kids Need:
Support

*

Support doesn't mean dependence.
Rather, it acknowledges that life isn't always easy,
and extends a warm hand of reassurance and assistance.

Use these words with your child often:

Let me be your shoulder to lean on.
You can count on me.
I'm here for you.
How can I help you?
I understand.
I'm ready to listen.
I'll stand by you.

Try It!
Let your child know that whatever situation
he gets into, even if sometimes embarrassing,
you are there for him.

All Kids Need:
Togetherness

*

Sometimes someone can live among lots of other people,
yet still feel isolated and alone.

Mark Twain said that
"When one really needs a friend,
it is too late to cultivate one."

Togetherness pays exponentially upon the time and energy
we invest in relationships with others.

Show your child – by example – the awesome pleasure it is to *matter* in
other people's lives, to be a part of their joys and sorrows, to think of
others and be thought of, to be counted on as a devoted and reliable
friend and "buddy" who sticks around through the ups and downs of life.

Help your child learn good social skills for bonding, caring,
sharing, and developing healthy relationships.

Try It!
**The next time your child gets into an argument
with someone, use that opportunity to develop the
skills of working things out peacefully.**

All Kids Need:
Tolerance & Understanding

*

No two human beings are alike.

Each person is made up of unique life experiences,
abilities and disabilities, strengths and weaknesses.

Each is a beautiful instrument that plays an
integral role in the orchestra of life.

Each and every human being
– man woman and child –
is important and significant.

Teach your child to respect differences, to appreciate diversity in
skin color, language, culture, ethnicity, and religious beliefs.
And to fight against prejudice, bigotry and hatred.

Teach your child to love all humanity, all life.

Try It!
**Read with your child the wonderful book, "A
Million Visions of Peace" by Garrison and Tubesing,
or other children's books on peace.**

All Kids Need:
Toys & Treats (...but not too many sweets)

*

The best toys are the ones that aren't just fun, but also develop:
imagination,
creativity,
coordination,
interpersonal skills,
patience,
and other important skills.

Encourage your local toy store to stock toys and games that develop such skills, and not only the ones that are commercially popular.

Foods with lots of refined sugar and caffeine promote hyperactivity, energy highs and lows, and mood swings. Allow them for your child in moderation; check food labels for nutritional information.

Try It!
Consider carob as an alternative to chocolate, and fruits as an alternative to candy.

All Kids Need:
Trust

*

Trust is a precious commodity that is not easily earned
yet can easily be lost.

If a family member, public official, or someone else known to your child
does something wrong, help your child understand on their level, and
work through their feelings of disappointment and betrayal.

If you made a mistake that caused weakening of your child's trust:
apologize,
explain,
ask forgiveness,
and make real changes to correct the wrong.

Appreciate that it might take a while to rebuild and repair.

Always be honest.

Be worthy of your child's trust.

Try It!
Make "trustworthiness," "integrity," "honesty", and
"honor," integral parts of your family's vocabulary.

All Kids Need:
Unconditional Love

*

When I served as a youth leader, a teen in my group confessed that he felt like an utter failure because he never would – or could – live up to his father's expectations. This teen showed an amazing knack for the electrical craft, but his father was a scholar who had high hopes that his son would follow in his footsteps of the academic world. The father told me, "If only he would try, he could make the grade." I asked, "When was the last time you told your son that you love him?" He answered sternly, "I don't need to tell him that; he knows it already."

Love is not something that is dependent on any grade or performance. Don't let pride or unfair expectations stop you from accepting your child for who he or she is.

Don't let your love for your child be only "presumed." Express your love with words. Show your love with actions. For is not love what it's all about!

Try It!
Tell your child today and tomorrow and every day "I Love You!"

All Kids Need:
Values, Ethics & Character

*

Some say that personality is what we are born with,
but character is what we learn and develop.
In any event, character is what makes us significant.

Character impacts on everything we do, on all of our relationships,
on our self-image and ultimately on what we contribute to the world.

Model and teach your child good character traits, such as:
Courage.
Honesty.
Friendship.
Kindness.
Truthfulness.
Compassion.
Restraint.
Fairness.
Integrity.
Honor.

Try It!
Create a chart of five good character traits,
and reinforce good character by adding stars
each time your child uses a particular trait.

All Kids Need:
Wholesome Friends

*

Peers have more influence on children than we might like to admit.

Don't simply choose your child's friends...
but teach your child the skills of discernment to pick good friends.

That way, she can also use good judgement in the future to pick
good boyfriends and girlfriends, good roommates, good co-workers,
good neighbors, and hopefully a good spouse!

Try It!
**Open a discussion with your child on
"What Makes a Good Friend?"**

All Kids Need:
X-tra Loving & Attention

*

Truth is, life is often tough.
We don't have all the answers.
We make mistakes.
Things get confusing.

When we give our children lots of love and attention,
we give them strength, courage and power
to get through anything.

Withholding love is like neglecting to water a flower.
Overdoting love is like over-watering it.
Healthy love is a fresh, flowing wellspring from which
our child can always draw nourishment.

Everyone shares the core needs: *to love* and *to be loved.*

In a world with healthy love, our children and all of humanity flourish.

Try It!
**The next time your child is feeling a bit "down,"
shower him with abundant love and affection.**

All Kids Need:
Yes
More Than No

*

No's are important.
Everyone needs rules, boundaries, standards.

But yes's are also important.

I do not promote permissiveness. Much of our popular culture is inundated with signs and symbols of "If it feels good, do it." The solid parent is the one who says, "Whatever goes on out there in society, here in this family and home, we have higher standards and values."

But this message is most effective when parents, guardians, caregivers and teachers highlight and accentuate the unlimited possibilities and positive opportunities in life, rather than only underscore the negative.

Try It!
The next time you need to "draw the line" of what can't be done, be sure to include creative suggestions of what *can* be done.

All Kids Need:

Zany Zebras with Purple Polkadots & Lots of Other Silly Things to Laugh About Together!

✳

Childhood is not forever. Life itself is not forever.

Cherish the moments you have together with your children and others that you love. Let laughter and good memories be abundant!

Let's celebrate the wonder of childhood and youth, and never have a shortage of love for the world's children. For children are the greatest treasure of life!

Try It!
Take lots of pictures throughout your child's life, and keep a scrapbook of memories and special times shared together.

Life's Greatest Treasures
by *Zimmy Zimberg*

Children are a precious gift,
An affirmation of the miracle of Life,
A glimpse of the sacred and pure.

But a delicate treasure they are:
So innocent, so dependent, so vulnerable.
They trust in us to keep them safe.

How then shall we care for these greatest of treasures?
With patience and nurturance,
With kindness, gentleness and compassion.

Make sure that their basic needs are provided for:
Healthy meals, proper clothing, and safe shelter.
Keep them cool in the Summer, warm in the Winter.

Comfort them when they cry, when they hurt.
Carry them when they are tired or weak.
Care for them when they are sick.

Protect them from harm.
Carefully choose in whose watch they are kept.
Be not silent when you witness *any* child abused or neglected.

Don't turn away from a child in need,
Even if he or she is not your own.
For we all suffer when we abdicate our responsibility to the young.

Don't let children walk blindly into unsafe territory.
Share your own life experiences as aged, tested wisdom,
Let them benefit from the lessons you have learned.

Yet, don't over-protect or push them to unreal expectations.
Rather, let each grow according to his or her individual self,
Each to their own pace and capacity, to their own unique nature.

Allow them to try, even to fall and make mistakes.
Allow them to accept consequences and learn responsibility.
When they fall, help them get up with renewed spirit.

Encourage them to dream, to play, to create, to feel.
Respect their attempts for individuality and independence –
Traits that will serve them well in our challenging world.

Listen to them and allow them to be heard; respect their opinions.
Don't coldly invalidate their thoughts or deny their feelings or fears.
Believe in them and help them believe in themselves.

Push for personal excellence, but never for perfection.
Reward sincere effort, irrespective of outcome.
Acknowledge that even "failures" are still valid attempts.

Read good stories, sing together, laugh together, learn together.
Enjoy the beauty of nature together.
Spend quality time together.

Encourage their questions, their curiosities.
Let no question be stupid or unaskable.
Don't be afraid to say, "I'm not sure, but that's a good question!"

Never be too proud to say, "I made a mistake."
Be quick to say "I'm sorry."
Always encourage communication and forgiveness.

Realize that, like adults, children have both better and worse days.
Always be patient.
Be abundant in forgiveness by looking not backward but forward.

Don't accentuate their disabilities or weaknesses.

Instead stress their abilities and strengths,
Who they *are* rather than who they are not.

Give unconditional love, praise and support.
For demeaning criticism is destructive,
While praise to children is like sunshine and water to flowers.

Help them build good character and virtue:
Responsibility, self discipline, honesty and compassion.
Let them learn from your sterling good example.

Teach them how to choose good friends,
And how to be a good friend.
Show them skills how to avoid negative influences.

Don't force or coerce faith,
Rather provide religious inspiration and moral consistency
That they will intuitively want to emulate.

Provide them with tools to be emotionally resilient.
Teach them skills to keep buoyant
Through the stormy waves we know life can sometimes bring.

Teach them not to deny the negative,
But to keep mostly focused on the positive.
Help them explore and feel life's refreshing wonders.

Help them to have courage in the face of challenge and handicap.
For those with especially sensitive souls,
Teach them to protect their vulnerabilities.

Sure, set limits and standards.
Provide structure, goals and appropriate discipline.
But always in gentle fairness and never in anger.

If you've had a particularly hard day, which we all do,

Let your frustration or anger cool.
Communicate to your child, "I'm having a difficult day today."

If you're feeling under pressure, don't take it out on a child.
Abuse and neglect – whether physical or emotional – is cruel.
Children are not dumping grounds for adults' problems.

If you have suffered abuse in your own childhood,
Defy those who abused by stopping the cycle of abuse, now.
Get professional and pastoral help, as needed, to heal and grow.

Let your child see parents who relate to each other with love.
Who share and give to one another without control,
Who resolve conflicts with respect, mutuality and affection.

Build a home of warmth, of wisdom, of faith, of love, of peace.
Let your voice – inside and outside the home – be gentle and kind,
Let your home be a hermitage of safe and joyous refuge.

Children are life's greatest treasures.
Not only for what they give us,
But also for the goodness within ourselves they help us discover.

Celebrate each child simply for who he or she is.
For every child is life itself,
In each child is our hope for a better tomorrow.

So, care well for these greatest treasures.
In doing so, children reconnect us to our own selves, our own souls.
Indeed, children reconnect us to God.

✳

Notes:

Reflections:

Keep Connected!

Zimmy's Parenting e-Newsletter:
If you are a parent, guardian or other caregiver, receive a free quarterly e-mail newsletter, filled with lots of great parenting ideas! Send an e-mail to: subscribeparent@zimmy.net

Zimmy's Professional e-Newsletter:
If you are an educator, social worker or other professional who works with children, youth and families, receive a free quarterly e-mail newsletter filled with lots of great program ideas, reports & resources. Send an e-mail to: subscribeprofessional@zimmy.net

"All Kids Need" Parent Support Groups:
Parents and other caregivers benefit greatly be sharing ideas and providing each other with support and encouragement. If you would like to receive free information on how to start and lead an "All Kids Need" parent support group in your community, send an e-mail to: akngroups@zimmy.net

Look for these Upcoming Books!
"Zimmy's Guide to What Love is About" (ISBN 1-92899-01-2) Feb 2001
"Zimmy's Guide to Preventing Child Abuse" (ISBN 1-928995-03-9) April 2001
"Zimmy's Guide to Teen Success" (ISBN 1-928995-02-0) September 2001

Share Your Experience!
Let's all learn from each other! Share your personal story, poem or insight about childrearing, working with kids & families, relationships, marriage, teen success, heroes, or other personal growth topics. If we publish your submission in an upcoming book or e-mail newsletter, you'll receive some nifty gifts from our catalog! Send via e-mail to: input@zimmy.net

Visit our Web Site!
www.zimmy.net

Life's Great! • 2565 Broadway PMB #137 • New York, NY 10025-5657

The two
greatest gifts
we give
our children
are
roots
&
wings

In Appreciation

When I think about all the special individuals who have warmly and magically enriched my life, I am filled with the deepest awe and gratitude. Some have been relatives, others friends and acquaintances, some have been teachers and mentors, others total strangers... each sharing their kindness and experience along the path of life. Among them, my thanks to:

David Richter for unconditional friendship. Maya Bendgi for hope. Lawrence Richards for coaching me to be my best. Randy Lazarus for inspiration. Steve Mernick for guidance. Lorna Valerio for her courageous example. Dr. Meshulum Teller and Susan Sullivan Cappi for understanding.

Chave Friedlander, my editor, for insight and friendship. Hope Vanderberg, Judy Schwartz, Levana Ruch and Norman Kabak for their very capable assistance. Karen Bell of K.B. Productions in Columbus, Ohio, the Ohio Department of Human Services, Mary Kozak, and the Blandin Foundation's Children First program, for helping launch this book. Sharon Castlen, John Kremer, Kate and Doug Bandos, Tami DePalma and Kim Dushinski, book marketers par excellence. Carolyn Hessel of JBC, who encouraged me to leave my former job to write books such as this.

My "Godparents," Jack and Lee Iden – childhood friends of my parents – who have always taken their role seriously by providing me with so much love. Gary Torgow, Arie Leibovitz, Marcus Rohtbart, Norman Goodman, and their families, for providing support and encouragement.

My Grandmother Bertha Mishcovsky, of blessed memory, and Grandmother Ida Zimberg, for modeling sterling character.

Finally, my dear parents, for their selfless love, wisdom, and for believing in the talents and unique abilities of each of their children and grandchildren.

To these, and many more unnamed, go my utmost thanks and blessings.

About the Author

✳

Avraham Zimmy Zimberg is a child advocate, guidance counselor, relationship specialist, and ordained rabbi. He holds a Masters of Education degree and has served in various capacities for national youth organizations.

He also is a composer, singer, musician, dancer and graphic artist. Audiences throughout the world are moved by his soulful performances, which weave songs, stories and folk guitar into a personal growth experience.

Zimmy draws practical wisdom from an eclectic mix of traditional sources, life experience, observation, making mistakes and learning from them ...and especially from listening. He enjoys nature and cinema and spends his spare time looking for a compassionate wife to build a loving home together.

He is sought after as a speaker on issues of children and youth, character education, relationships and conflict resolution, and as a facilitator of life skills workshops for youth, parents and professionals.

If you'd like Zimmy to be an inspiring part of your organization's next conference or your school's next motivational assembly, contact him at:

Zimmy Zimberg
Life's Great!
2565 Broadway PMB #137
New York, NY 10025-5657

1-877-39-GREAT
info@zimmy.net